Making Money Online

50 Easy Ways To Make Money Online From Home

(Entrepreneur, Internet Marketing, Passive Income)

by Frank Hunter

© 2016 Frank Hunter
All Rights Reserved

Table of Contents

Table of Contents

Introduction

Chapter 1 – Ways to Make Money Online: Get Paid to Review Products

Chapter 2 – Sell Used Books Online and Make Money

Chapter 3 – Earn Money by Reading Emails: How Does It Work and How Do I Earn?

Chapter 4 – Got An Online Business? Start A Blog

Chapter 5 – Start Your Own Smart Phone App Design Business

Chapter 6 – How To Make Money Answering Questions Online

Chapter 7 – How To Freelance For Profit

Chapter 8 – Writing Articles For Money - Your Step-By-Step Guide To Get Paid To Write Articles

Chapter 9 – Paid Per Click - Get A Higher Return Of Investment

Chapter 10 – Making Money With Online Micro Jobs

Chapter 11 – Make Money Online With Revenue Sharing Site

Chapter 12 – Get Paid For Market Research

Chapter 13 – Ways to Making Money Through Stock Photography

Chapter 14 – Twitter Sponsored Tweets: Making Money With Twitter

Chapter 15 – How to Sell Your Unused Clothes Online

Chapter 16 – Online Private Loans: A Discreet Alternative

Chapter 17 – Affiliate marketing

Chapter 18 – Email marketing

Chapter 19– Internet marketing

Chapter 20– How To Use Cost Per Action To Make Money

Chapter 21 – How You Can Earn Money From Home by Writing Reviews

Chapter 22 – Ways To Make Online Stock Trading Simpler

Chapter 23 – Matched Betting

Chapter 24 – How to Make a Website Earn Money

Chapter25 – Make Money Writing For the Web on Content Sites

Chapter 26 – Gleaning Traffic From Big Name Sites

Chapter 27 – Become An Online Tutor!

Chapter 28 – Mystery Shopping Online

Chapter 29 – How to Make Money Posting Videos Online

Chapter 30 – Maximizing Profit From Fiverr And Other Gig Marketplaces

Chapter 31 – Rent out a room

Chapter 32 – Turn your home into a vacation rental

Chapter 33 – Rent storage space

Chapter 34 – Rent your parking space

Chapter 35 – How To Make Money With Kindle Publishing

Chapter 36– Mobile Phone Recycling

Chapter37 – Get A Part Time Job Online And Increase Your Income

Chapter 38– Make a Living Selling DVDs and Video Games on eBay

Chapter 39 – Tell Client Success Stories To Win Business And Make More Money

Chapter 40 – Buying and Selling Domains to Make Money

Chapter 41 – Sell Your Travel Photos

Chapter 42 – Online Money Saving - Making the Most Out of Your Earnings

Chapter 43 – Make Money Writing For the Web on Job Boards

Chapter 44 – Benefits of Online Ordering for Restaurant Delivery Services

Chapter 45– Start A Home Based Business By Providing Dog Walking Services

Chapter 46 – How to Make Extra Money Online With Getting Paid to Sites

Chapter 47 – Get Paid to Be Online

Chapter 48 – Online Competitions - How to Make Money From It

Chapter 49 – Become an Uber Partner Driver

Chapter 50 – Downloading Apps

Conclusion

Disclaimer

While all attempts have been made to verify the information provided in this book, the author does not assume any responsibility for errors, omissions, or contrary interpretations of the subject matter contained within. The information provided in this book is for educational and entertainment purposes only. The reader is responsible for his or her own actions and the author does not accept any responsibilities for any liabilities or damages, real or perceived, resulting from the use of this information.

Introduction

Making money online is not all that big of a secret. The truth is anyone can conceivably become financially independent. All it takes is for you to follow a few simple steps and repeat them every day until you reach your goal.

You have to start somewhere and here is the foundation for a successful career making money online. These only have to be done once or twice, and you will be on your way to collecting income that will soon have you living your dream. The fist thing you need is a website that is eye-catching and user-friendly.

To get this, you need to purchase a domain name. This is the most important step of all. The domain name has to be in tune with what you are offering and also with the keywords that search engines use to locate products. If you are not comfortable designing your website you can use a website builder or even buy a made to order website.

Now comes the part that makes money come in. Its called content, clear and simple. You have to have content that is interesting, informative and also search engine ready.

They have to include the key words or phrases that will get them noticed by the search engines when people are looking for the item you are selling.

Some people like to the right the articles themselves, but you can outsource this work as well. This may be better if you are unfamiliar with Search Engine Optimization techniques.

Next, comes the part that is so much fun. You can find affiliates and ebooks for free online that you can promote from your very own website.

Affiliates give you a percentage of all sales that originate from your site, and the ebooks are pure profit. A lot of people will attempt this portion first, but it is important not of put the "cart before the horse."

Finally, it is time to build your links. You should use some opt in form on your site connected with a newsletter this will give you email addresses of people who are interested in what you have to say.

If you are serious about making money online find a person who has become the success you are trying to become.

Imitation is the sincerest form of flattery, and the person you choose will be more than glad to have you duplicate that success, in the end, your success is their success as well.

If you follow these steps and be persistent and consistent in your pursuit of success, you will not find it hard to achieve this goal. Making money online is a formula, but there is nothing secret about.

If your dream is to be wealthy learning how to use the tool called the Internet properly will get you there quicker than playing the Lottery. If you apply yourself, you can get all that you want and more.

Chapter 1 – Ways to Make Money Online: Get Paid to Review Products

Paid review sites are a great way to make money online. You can make a living writing reviews for virtually any product available on the market. When it comes to buying a product or service, reviews play a key role for many consumers.

You can get paid to review websites, electronics, home appliances, cell phones, businesses, books and millions of other products.

One of the easiest ways to supplement your income is to set up a website or blog, choose a niche, and then review products related to your niche. Product reviews can be stand-alone or comparative.

The goal of most people when they write a review is to share their opinion with the world about a specific product. A review that is written by someone who has tested the product will attract more attention than one written by someone who is not familiar with that product.

You can take a photo of the product yourself, use a picture of you using it, or use an image from the merchant's website.

If you post reviews on your site or blog, make sure you include an image and video of the product that you are writing about.

You may also collect information about different products from your family and friends. The structure of a review is simple, containing an introduction, overview, and summary.

Chapter 2 – Sell Used Books Online and Make Money

Used books are all over and finding great prices to buy used books can be done if you try. Many times people will give their used books away once they are done with them.

Go to places as flea markets, consignment stores, charity shops or online auctions or even approach family and friends to find used books. When you purchase the used book for resale, remember not to overpay.

Unless this is a valuable book, use $1.00 as a ceiling price. Keep in mind that you might have to offer free shipping depending on your competition.

Chapter 3 – Earn Money by Reading Emails: How Does It Work and How Do I Earn?

Earning by reading emails is one of the many online money generating jobs that have been used by many for quite some time now.

The great popularity and necessity of the internet have really increased in recent years, and with the bad economy, more and more people are trying to find ways to get more income running on their bank accounts.

With the help of the email reading jobs, you can easily drive a nice amount of money by reading emails. But how does it work? What should you know? What are the risks?

There are so many questions that you should be aware of but let us first understand the mystery behind this online scheme.

Chapter 4 – Got An Online Business? Start A Blog

In today's online business world today it is important for online entrepreneurs to start a blog. A blog generates awareness for your products and services and educates prospects so that they become future customers.

Why Start a Blog?

When you start a blog, it makes it possible for you to generate interest for your products and services. The more frequently you post, the more often the search engine spiders will check out your website.

Your blog will begin to draw in traffic to your website which, in turn, will help you to sell your products or services.

Making Money From Your Blog

There are several money-making opportunities you can have on your blog. This include:

Google AdSense where you display advertisements on your blog. You are paid each time a viewer click on an ad.

Selling Advertising such as online banner ads that appear on your blog to businesses who want to reach your readers.

Affiliate Marketing where you promote other people's products or services that are relevant to your blog topic. The product owner will pay you a commission when somebody buys via your affiliate link.

Electronic books or reports that you can create yourself and sell on your website.

Chapter 5 – Start Your Own Smart Phone App Design Business

Let's face it... any mobile device is only as good as the software that drives it. To get the most out of those smart phones, users need apps that they can access quickly and easily, giving them the ability to do everything from getting directions to find a nearby restaurant.

For businesses, it is essential that they be able to connect with customers on the fly so that they can be successful.

Between those two lies the domain of the IT professional. This is where having a smart phone app design business can pay off for you. Because, while they may understand the need for a good app, most businesses aren't able to design one for themselves.

They need someone who can both understand their needs and utilise the necessary technology to create an effective app.

As an app designer, you need to be aware of current trends in apps so that you can integrate successful design strategies for your clients. You also need to have a broad knowledge of various programming languages so that you can choose the right one to use for each app that you design.

This shows your clients that you are listening to their needs and creating an app tailored to their expectations.

Chapter 6 – How To Make Money Answering Questions Online

Suppose you are excellent at your hobby and you want to help others and potentially get money for doing so. There is a business model for that: Answering questions for money.

On top of generating income, this can also serve to help you create a public reputation as an expert, which can aid you with your career progression or other opportunities. Here I will share some ideas that will serve to help you to be successful at generating income answering questions.

Your profile is your pamphlet:

Do not be greedy

Prove that you know what you claim to know

Drive traffic

Don't hasten your responses

Chapter 7 – How To Freelance For Profit

How can you freelance for profit is truly a loaded question? It truly requires some thought and firm attention to detail on the part of the prospective online worker. Many would say that it involves some steps.

These steps have to be constantly reevaluated through the course of your Internet working career. But first, let's define what it means to be a freelancer.

A person that is choosing to become part of the freelancing world is someone that is making the decision to attempt to utilise their skills with the latest technology and turn themselves into a virtual worker.

So basically they are taking any talents that they have that translate into something that has to do with computer skills-plus and offering it up to an employer for payment.

By the addition of the plus, it is understood that you need the computer skills period, but then you can add more to these skills to open up more markets.

Chapter 8 – Writing Articles For Money - Your Step-By-Step Guide To Get Paid To Write Articles

If your goal is to start writing articles for money, follow this step-by-step guide. It will show you how to get paid to write articles.

Step #1: Define Your Goal

What do you want to obtain from your writings? Do you plan to quit your day-job? Or only make a few extra hundred dollars per months? Before you even get started, you should know what your goal is. Alternatively, your aim will miss. You'll be like a ship adrift, whirling from coast to coast, using a lot of energy, but getting nowhere.

Step #2: Learn About Article Writing

Before I started my career as a full-time professional writer, I learnt a lot about the profession. I invested in courses; I borrowed books; I read, and I wrote a lot. You should read as many high-quality articles, as you can find.

Get at least one good course about how to start writing articles for money. Personally, I have several in my arsenal that I keep going back to, and either re-read or re-watch the videos. This is a business where you should keep learning and keep writing.

Step #3: Think Out Of The Box

Maybe you thought that the only way to get paid to write articles was by selling them? Well, it's not. Far from that. You can make money from your articles in several ways:

1: Put them on your home page, and make money either from ads or affiliate products.

2: Submit them to article directories, and point them to an affiliate product, or your squeeze page to start your list of subscribers.

3: Sell them to other marketers - but before you do that, you should make a name for yourself, so people will realise that they are buying quality. Or they'll pay you less than $2 per article. Even if you can spit out eight articles per hour, that means that you'll make around $12 per hour, which is not a lot.

Step #4: Target Your Articles, Before You Write Them

Before you write an article, define its purpose so that you can write it the best way. There's a big difference between articles meant to be put on a home site, and an article that should get you back links, and an article that's meant to send traffic to your site. If you want the best performance from your article, you have to target it.

Chapter 9 – Paid Per Click - Get A Higher Return Of Investment

There are plenty of different search engines being used by men and women all over the world that utilise different keywords that match the queries of these people.

The idea of PPC or Pay Per Click pertains to purchasing links that can be found on a results page. Businesses that use this online advertising strategy often hire a company or group of people to handle it for them.

They make certain that their client will be able to accumulate a lot of traffic through their adverts to gain more profit.

As the name suggests, a certain amount is paid per click you get that leads a client to your website. A lot of companies worldwide use this campaign management to further their business in the online world.

If you intend on making your advertising campaign a profitable endeavour, make a list of objectives that you want your organisation to achieve within a set time frame.

There should be a proper format to follow when planning a campaign; these include things such as website selection, choosing the right keywords, and acquisition point.

Come up with a banner that is appealing and incorporates the keywords that will attract potential clients into clicking on them. Together with other SEO (search engine optimisation) tools, you will be able to make the most of your Pay Per Click campaign.

Chapter 10 – Making Money With Online Micro Jobs

Most businesses today choose to outsource tasks rather than hiring in-house personnel because it helps save time and money. Not only this, many choose to use freelancers offering micro jobs, online services for $5, as it is an opportunity to get quality services at an affordable price.

Speaking from a seller's point of view, it is an excellent platform to give your freelancing business a firm grounding in the industry. Some individuals have paid off house loans and adopted children using their income from such freelance job platforms.

If you're a freelancer looking to capitalise on the popularity of online services for $5, there are a few insider secrets that will make you success on such job platforms. Here's how to attract clients for your gig services.

Micro Job sites are free to join. However, they charge a certain percentage of your total earnings or a flat fee per job. The standard rate is $1 commission for every $5 job.

Chapter 11 – Make Money Online With Revenue Sharing Site

Are you searching for opportunities for making money online? If so, you must have come across various revenue sharing sites. These sites offer their members share of the advertising revenue they generate for contribution to a website, forum or blog.

The work involved in revenue sharing is very simple. You add value to a site, each time you write an article or post a comment. Likewise, the site will generate money by way of advertising revenue, shown on the page wherein your information is being displayed.

Profit Sharing is great for people who take pleasure in writing, blogging or commenting since it implies that you essentially are paid for contributions you made.

Although the essence of spelling and grammar are important elements but still you do not need to be an extremely talented or a gifted. You just need to have the aptitude to write about the things you are passionate about.

Chapter 12 – Get Paid For Market Research

If you think you are up for market research jobs, then there is good news for you - this is job pays you handsomely. You get to draw an average annual income of 61k and if you can make it big in here - you will be able to earn as much as 112k a year, just like some top professionals are already doing.

So if you have secured a bachelor's degree in marketing, you can seriously consider opting for this career. A master's degree in the same field is sure to further your cause as well.

Apart from these elementary degrees, what you actually need to possess is an ability to grasp situations quickly. You need to be blessed with good analytical skills too.

This is because market research basically involves feeling the pulse of the consumers and deciding beforehand, based on the collected statistical data, whether a product or a commodity to be launched will be received well by the people or be out rightly rejected.

Based on the key findings other important decisions such as advertising strategies too are formulated. This is why market research wing of every company is a treasured unit of the organization.

Chapter 13 – Ways to Making Money Through Stock Photography

Before we look at how to make money through this hobby, let us find understand what stock photography is. It is the availability of photographs which are licensed for specific usage. You would be amazed at how much demand there is of stock photographs.

They are required by graphic and website designers, internet advertising agencies and publishing companies. The best thing about stock photography is that you don't have to be professionally qualified to make money through this means. All it takes is an interest in photography coupled with creativity.

Gradually you will develop the knack to market yourself successfully and hence end up making money too!

Now some people may argue that stock photography pays very little regarding individual photographs. But those who whine about this are viewing it as a case of 'a glass being half full'.

It is true that stock photos are sold for as low as $1. But the fact of the matter is that many people can use a particular photograph. Couple this with the fact that the same photograph can be put up on several sites.

A quick math will reveal that this is a sure way to make a tidy sum of money! Nowadays you find that some people are making a living from stock photography such is its vast potential of making money.

Now how does one actually go about making money through stock photography? Here are a few things you should do to get started. The most obvious step is to commence with building your own unique collection of photographs.

Try to incorporate a sense of novelty in the kind of pictures and angles you capture. You should think about the range of collection you wish to build. Some people like to concentrate on a particular theme and be a niche provider. Others like to cover a whole spectrum of themes. The choice is entirely yours.

The next step to making money with stock photography is to open an account with the online stock photography websites. Now those companies who accept photographs from a wide range of photographers (including amateurs and hobbyists) are called Microstock photography companies. They operate on a low price high volume game.

There are some prominent microstock sites such as ShutterStock.com, BigStockPhoto.com, Fotolia.com, 123rf.com and Dreamstime.com. You can open an account with some of them. After this, you create a sample folder. This is your time to showcase your talent and get selected.

Choose a few of your best photographs and upload them. Here's a useful tip. Make sure the photographs you upload are accompanied with a short and relevant title. This can help those searching for photographs find relevant ones quickly.

Chapter 14 – Twitter Sponsored Tweets: Making Money With Twitter

Twitter Sponsored Tweets, also known as just Sponsored Tweets, offers a way for advertisers to broadcast their tweets across the profiles of high-profile celebrities or regular accounts that have some followers. How does it work?

Well here's a good way to look at it. If you're the tweeter, then you get paid for broadcasting Sponsored Tweets on your profile whenever an advertiser chooses your profile as one they want to advertise on.

The more followers you have (and the more they pay attention to what you tweet about), the more success you'll have in making Sponsored Tweets work for you.

However, if you're the advertiser, you pay money to celebrities, Web Celebs or popular tweeters for hosting your ads on their profiles.

For instance, stars like Stephanie Pratt of "The Hills" make over $2,000.00 per tweet because they have a high clout with their followers. You know that when Stephanie posts a tweet, her followers will take her word on the product, click the link and likely make a purchase.

But if you don't have that much money, you can choose advertisers that are much less well known that are happy to tweet for only a few dollars - or less.

With Sponsored Tweets, you can get a good idea right out the gate of who you

Chapter 15 – How to Sell Your Unused Clothes Online

Selling your unused clothing online can be a pleasurable way to make yourself some extra money. Not only that but it provides you with a chance to be utterly ruthless in what you give away and keep, while at the same time making space for any "new seasons" purchases you might be wanting to make!

One of the most important things to do is to make sure whatever you're selling still has its tags left on. This is the biggest source of proof that you haven't worn the clothes at all.

To make use of secondary market websites such as eBay, it's important that you makes sure you give a detailed account of each garment you are going to sell and provide a set of well-lit pictures to go with them.

If at all possible, take photos of the clothes either hung up against a white or light coloured background.

Chapter 16 – Online Private Loans: A Discreet Alternative

People with bad credit do not always have a lot of options when they are in need of money for an unforeseen expense.

Generally, those with good credit ratings will simply ask their home bank for an unsecured personal loan and they will generally end up with favorable terms and reasonable monthly payments.

This is not the case for borrowers with bad credit, however. These people often need to avail the use of private loan options. Therefore, there is a need for additional services specifically designed for time when, despite bad credit, a quick personal loan is needed.

Private Loans

Strictly speaking, a private loan is any loan offered by an individual to another individual (also called peer-to-peer lending).

Discretion Is Key

If you need money for an unexpected expense, maybe car repair or a traffic ticket, finding the cash right away can be difficult.

Online Private Loan Statistics

Since the degree of risk will vary from borrower to borrower, the terms of these private loans will vary as well. Generally, you can borrow as little as $100 and up to $5,000 at different interest rates and fees.

A Good Solution

In the case when you need money and have no other means to get it, use of online private loans give bad credit borrowers a good solution to their problems.

Though the terms of these loans can be rather strict and the interest rates high due to your bad credit and risk, if you have no other choice, they are a viable tool to help you in times of need.

Chapter 17 – Affiliate marketing

This is among the most popular online marketing techniques out there. Affiliate marketing works on a trade-for-trade basis and is generally considered to be a risk-free method.

This is so because, the company or business that is advertising their product does not have to pay the advertising charges unless a successful conversion rate happens.

Affiliate marketing is normally known as pay-per-click sales or pay-per-view adverts in layman's terms. The advertisement aims to appeal the customer into buying a product, signing up at a website, or viewing content.

As far as the conversion rate matters, the effectiveness of the advertisement is measured through a unique code embedded in the links. This code can be tracked and used to measure conversions.

Chapter 18 – Email marketing

When the kinds of online marketing initiated, many of the conversions were made through email marketing. A method by which an email is sent to a list of people hoping to sell them your product is email marketing.

This is done in order get the prospective customer understand your product. However, this method has lost its effectiveness since most email services come with a spam filter, making it harder to spread the word across and makes audience highly limited.

Moreover, such methods are generally ill-perceived from the general masses, since they have been known to be associated with spam. As the case with affiliate marketing, the payments for such source of advertisements is not made until there is a conversation rate that proves the effectiveness.

There have also been reports of email marketing being banned in some countries, and the last thing any advertising company wants to face is a lawsuit slammed to their faces.

Email marketing is considered effective because email marketing is cost effective, it is easy to keep track of your data, the work can be automated, your sales improves and also because it is quick to yield results.

Chapter 19– Internet marketing

Surveys have shown that this is by far the most popular form of advertising according to the latest trends. Emails can be blocked through a spam guard and all leading web browsers come with advertisement blockers, so it is no surprise that there was a third alternate figured out to get the job done.

This form of advertising is highly dependent on search engines to get the job done. A few ways of making money online are.

SMS Premium: One of the trusted companies to offer this kind of job is Recursos Moviles.

Blog creation: You can be an affiliate marketer and sell products if you own a blog. You can also get leads by asking for the visitor's for their email addresses. The only consideration is that you need a product to sell. Well, even if you do not have a product of your own, you can choose one that interests you from affiliate promoting websites.

Chapter 20– How To Use Cost Per Action To Make Money

There are so many ways to make money on the internet. Everyone should be able to make some money with the internet. Even if it's writing articles for other people, marketing or just doing some odd jobs on Fiverr.com or something. One of the most common and sought after ways of making money online is through cost per action.

Cost per action marketing is one of the most sought after methods of making money online because there is no selling involved. All you do is just supply leads to the company of choice and then get paid. However, there is one catch. You have to be approved and selected by one of the CPA networks online.

Chapter 21 – How You Can Earn Money From Home by Writing Reviews

If you have a skill at reviewing, you could make cash online. Whether it is reviewing movies, books, or even large screen televisions, if you can review it, you can profit from your skills.

There are a few ways to do it. We are going to take a quick look at all of them. After that, it's up to you to continue the search. Ready to go?

Make Money From Home Writing Reviews

These are the basic ways you can make money with reviews online.

Sell

Publish

Chapter 22 – Ways To Make Online Stock Trading Simpler

A lot of people want to do online stock trading but unless you know how it works then it is tough to do. Trust me when I say that setting up a trade for some time down the road is a great way to make money and for a lot of investors that is their strategy.

What I would highly recommend doing is to put more money into stocks right now since the prices are somewhat low and history shows us that the price always goes up.

With more and more people worried about their portfolios and selling their stocks for way less than they should, it is time for you to step in and take this money making opportunity off their hands.

This is what I try to do every time the market drops and time and time again I keep on making money.

What you need to understand is that during a huge upswing you can make a lot of money and very quickly too

Chapter 23 – Matched Betting

Using the technique of matched betting, and a bit of knowledge, a clever person can make money from a bet regardless of the outcome of the event.

The bettor will use one of the free bets as the stake money and invest their money in a matching bet on the opposite outcome.

That is, the bettor uses the free bet to back and his or her money to lay on the outcome. Betting to win on one side and betting to lose on the other can earn online bucks for the smart bettor.

There are hundreds of bookmaker sites opening every day, so the potential to earn bucks by matched betting is virtually unlimited.

Chapter 24 – How to Make a Website Earn Money

There are many factors to consider when creating or running a website and online business, but in a commercial world, the most important question of all is how to make a website earn money and how to make it work for you rather than you work for it.

And the focus of this is to introduce you to a different approach to making money online and exactly how to make a website earn money for you.

Because as well as overcoming the challenge of presenting products to the world online and then driving traffic to your site, the absolute goal of your entire venture is to understand how to make a website earn money for you quickly, efficiently and effectively.

Chapter 25 – Make Money Writing For the Web on Content Sites

Many content sites will either pay for your articles directly or offer you a revenue sharing plan. They will give you a platform to publish your articles and help you gain visibility in the search engines.

Some content sites will allow other websites or ezines to reprint your articles depending on the rights you grant.

Because different content sites have different payment plans, you should read the terms of use closely to understand how you will be paid and what rights you have to reprint your articles elsewhere.

Chapter 26 – Gleaning Traffic From Big Name Sites

Getting web traffic from big name sites will take your online business to a higher level. It will allow you to make money fast and easy online.

Here are some of the sites you can glean web traffic from:

*Amazon.com

*Epinions.com

*Yahoo! Answers

*AllExperts.com

*Answerbag.com

*Ask Metafilter

Each of these sites allows visitors to interact in some way as part of a larger community. Amazon, for example, allows registered Amazon.com members to post their reviews of books, music, and other products. Sites like Yahoo! Answers and Answerbag.com are totally user-driven.

Chapter 27 – Become An Online Tutor!

Nine to five jobs can be mundane and tiring to put up with, online jobs such as affiliate marketing or web designing require special skills, taking online surveys can take up too much of your time, so in such a situation what can you do to make money online without spending too much of your time?

The answer is you become an online tutor.

Do you enjoy sharing or imparting knowledge to people but don't have anyone to call your 'student'? If you have trouble finding students to tutor in your neighborhood then why not resort to the internet?

The internet has revolutionized our way of working and now anyone can earn a substantial amount of money through the internet and from the convenience of one's home.

Chapter 28 – Mystery Shopping Online

Mystery shopping online is gaining more popularity as a tool worked by firms to check the quality of their goods and service providing, a raising amount of ads for this shopping are now found in newspapers and online.

It is the best method to make some additional money, but there are certain things that you want to understand prior you enter into it.

First, you want to get free time and a flexible schedule when you like to make additional money from this shopping.

This is the main reasons why a lot of mystery shoppers like to remain at home mothers or students who possess the time to do the shops.

This shows that you get a good opportunity of being assigned stores that are urgent or emergencies particularly when you first begin out as a shopper in mystery shop. Seriously check your skills when planning to do a mystery shopping online.

Internet access is essential because is access to a digital scanner or a fax machine to send the receipts to the industry you are employing for. Along with this, you will be asked to submit the written reports of your thoughts.

1. Get reimbursement

2. Understand the method

Chapter 29 – How to Make Money Posting Videos Online

Do you know that you can make money by posting videos online?

One of the places where you can earn money by posting original videos is Youtube.com. You can apply to join their partnership program. But you have to make sure that you own full rights to the videos that you submitted.

They will first look at the amount of videos being also submitted the total views before deciding if you're suitable for their partner program.

However, there are 2 sites that you might not know about, and I'm going to share these 2 sites with you.

1. Make Money Posting Videos On Revver.com

- Revver.com is a video sharing network pretty much like Youtube.com. They run based on a revenue sharing model where you can make money posting your videos.

2. Break.com Will Pay Up To $2000 For Awesome Videos

The other website that you can try is break.com. Break.com is a site that showcases funny and amusing videos and pictures. You can upload your videos and pictures all day long.

Chapter 30 – Maximizing Profit From Fiverr And Other Gig Marketplaces

Fiverr.com is a huge online marketplace where thousands of people trade their products or services for $5 - that's why it's called Fiverr.

Many people go to this site hoping to outsource some tasks related to their websites such as link building, web page design, WP install, etc., for a very affordable price, of course, because everything is sold for only 5 bucks!!

Not only website related products/services, but you can also find various products/service since there is almost no limitation, just use your imagination, and if you find something that you think could attract people's interest then you can sell it there!

It doesn't have to be something serious or difficult, as long as you think that it's something you can sell then you can sell it.

Chapter 31 – Rent out a room

Renting out a room can bring in several hundred extra dollars per month. This can make a huge difference in your finances. Just $500 a month turns into $6,000 per year. It doesn't take long to add up.

I know most people like their space but you can also be creative with this. Are you able to partition off a portion of the house?

Maybe add a kitchenette and laundry? What changes would it require to provide the privacy for an extra roommate or family? Depending on the layout and size of your home, this may be something to consider.

Chapter 32 – Turn your home into a vacation rental

Depending on your area, it may be beneficial to rent out your home as a vacation rental. Most think of a vacation rental as a mansion with a tennis court and in-ground pool, but reality is they come in all shapes and sizes.

If you have a mansion you wish to rent out, you'll simply charge more than you would if you're renting a small home in town. Nevertheless, this can be a lucrative option for most homeowners.

So how much can you rent your home for? Start by looking online at other vacation rentals in your area. What are they charging? This will give you an idea as to how much you can charge as well as the demand for vacation rentals within your area.

So where do you stay if you rent out your home? Well, like I said you have to be creative. I know of people who stay in their motor-home in a local park or stay with a friend or family member. Be creative and start generating some cash.

Chapter 33 – Rent storage space

Do you have extra room to store a car/motorhome/boat/misc.? Well then rent it to someone. Simply prepare the space and put an ad on Craigslist or the local classifieds. You may be surprised by the response. People don't always have the room for their stuff. So take advantage of this and make some extra cash.

Chapter 34 – Rent your parking space

Again, like any other cash-generating method, this depends on where you live. But for some homeowners, this may be a viable option. Is parking hard to come by where you live? Do you have a spare parking space? If you do..it could serve as a great little source of income.

Chapter 35 – How To Make Money With Kindle Publishing

Publishing on Kindle is not different from marketing any eBooks over the Internet. Although Amazon has a huge reputation on the market and offers great optimization features, there is still a need for the promotion to be set up by the author.

Buying reviews is not the best option; first of all, because Amazon filters professional reviewers out, secondly because of the credibility.

However, getting genuine reviews and giving away information while pointing to the product through article marketing and press releases is an effective way of making money with Kindle Publishing.

Chapter 36– Mobile Phone Recycling

Mobile phone recycling is a fantastic way to earn extra money when you're struggling for cash. There are also ways you can use old mobile phones to donate to charity. I've written the following this to explain how you can get cash for mobile phones by recycling and how it can benefit different people. The method of payment from the recycling are the following options-

- BACs

- Cheque

- Vouchers

Don't forget to give correct bank details when giving them to the company so you get the cash.

Chapter 37 – Get A Part Time Job Online And Increase Your Income

Looking for ways to increase your income online? You can easily boost your personal income by getting a part time job on the Internet. Are there really opportunities out there that will help you make real cash?

The truth is, the money making opportunities are there. But they may require specific skills. The type of jobs that are available.

1) Filling in surveys.

2) Freelance writing opportunities.

3) Affiliate marketing.

Chapter 38– Make a Living Selling DVDs and Video Games on eBay

Once you get up and running, selling DVDs and video games on eBay is a very easy way to make a living, but it does take a lot of initial groundwork.

There is a lot to consider such as where do I get my cheap DVDs?, what is the best way to advertise DVDs on eBay? How should I post them and how do I keep track of my finances?

Selling DVDs on eBay is easy and does not require a lot of brain power but once your store is up and running your day to day work schedule will have to involve the following...

* Reconciling the previous day's sales and profit/loss accounts

* Answering questions and inquiries from eBay customers.

* Fulfilling drop ship orders to eBay customers from retailers

* Posting manual eBay orders

* Updating prices and availability on your eBay adverts

* Adding to your eBay shop inventory

Although all of the above is relatively easy, selling on eBay is time-consuming and can easily take 8 hours a day. Customers on eBay do expect first class customer service and rapid response to inquiries, so it is worthwhile investing in a Blackberry or PDA phone. This allows you to send and receive emails on the go and was a lifeline for me as I preferred to work in the evenings and enjoy my days out with my kids.

If you are not prepared to put in at least 7-8 hours a day for the first couple of months and 3-4 hours a day when you are up and running, selling DVDs on eBay may not be the business for you. If you are money motivated, a fast learner and like the idea of working from home at times to suit you, get yourself ready to make a living out of selling DVDs on eBay.

The best selling DVDs on eBay are recent blue ray movies and Disney DVDs.

Chapter 39 – Tell Client Success Stories To Win Business And Make More Money

Effective marketing involves engaging potential customers with the value of what you offer. Most people don't naturally do this though. We tend to tell people about the features or process of our product or service.

Maybe we do this in an attempt to prove that we offer something of real substance. Whatever the reason, we don't grab people's attention in this way.

The thing is that most people aren't interested in features and process, at least not at first. In fact, a lot of people can be put off by too much of this sort of thing.

A great way of demonstrating value is through telling stories, and the best stories are told by the people who have been there before. Think about the reviews from previous customers that you get with online shopping sites.

These stories are great for demonstrating the value of products and can be far more useful than technical specifications in deciding what to buy.

The trick here then is to have a few client success stories you can share with potential clients. Ask your clients what difference you made to them, their teams and their business bottom line.

Dig down to get to the juicy bits about the value of your services. Then write the stories up and use them in your marketing. Put them on your website, have potted versions you can tell to potential clients you meet, use them in presentations, build your marketing strategy around your client success stories.

Chapter 40 – Buying and Selling Domains to Make Money

You may not know about it, but there is an entire world of domain traders who make millions of dollars buying and selling domain names. They are called "domainers" and the activity is called "domaining."

They usually lurk beneath the radar until some huge sale such as the sale of Candy.com for $3M catches the attention of the mainstream press.

The truth is, there is tons of money to be made in domain trading, and one of the most prominent entrepreneurs in the world - Bill Gates - has even gone on record to say that domain names will appreciate in value faster than any commodity known to man.

Chapter 41 – Sell Your Travel Photos

Taking pictures while you travel is a must for almost anybody these days. So why don't you also make money while you travel by selling your travel photos that you have taken? Well, this article will show you some dos and don'ts that hopefully will show you how you can effectively make money while you travel.

Here are some pointers that you can take note of the next time you take pictures of the places that you visit so that they are of the right quality that you can make some money selling them online.

1. Photo resolution should be at least 2200 x 1700 pixel.

2. The format of a photo should be JPEG for most online websites to accept.

3. The photo should not contain Company Names, Brand Names, Product Names, Date or Trademark.

4. If it is a photo of a distinct property or interior of the property, you must obtain written permission from the owner.

5. If it contains recognizable people, you must get "Model Release" and upload such document with your photo.

6. Only very partial nudity may be allowed.

7. Prepare pertinent "keywords" that you will have to include to make it easy for potential buyers to find your photo.

8. Lastly and most important of all, you MUST be the photographer.

Chapter 42 – Online Money Saving - Making the Most Out of Your Earnings

For years now shoppers have tried to save money one way or the other, it's now becoming easier with the availability of comparison sites, voucher code sites, and cash-back incentive sites as well as money-saving forums and blogs. Knowing where to look seems to be a bit of a minefield. Let's have a look at some of the available money-saving resources.

Comparison Sites

Comparison sites check through lots of retailers to find the lowest online prices. Using an automated service they visit many retailers collecting prices and delivery charges then collate them together to provide a list of prices normally listed from the cheapest first.

Voucher Sites

There's a lot of various discount code sites that can get you vouchers for various shops; many of the voucher directories list vouchers for a percentage of the listed prices, codes for free delivery, maybe a gift or offers such as buy one get one free, 2 for 1 etc.

Cashback sites

Cashback sites are specialist websites that pay a portion of the referral fee back to the person doing the shopping online. You simply have to register to the cashback site then choose the store that you wish to purchase from by clicking through one of the links to the store provided by the site.

Chapter 43 – Make Money Writing For the Web on Job Boards

Job boards allow freelancers to bid on writing jobs (usually ghostwriting jobs.) Job boards will connect you with clients but are also competitive. Make sure you understand the scope of a job before you bid, so you do not lock yourself into a situation that will not make you enough money to be worth your time.

Just as with content sites, you should read the terms of use so you understand your pay and whether the job board will keep a commission. One thing to understand - usually after the job is done, you are not permitted to work with a client without paying the job board a commission.

Chapter 44 – Benefits of Online Ordering for Restaurant Delivery Services

What is a Restaurant Delivery Service?

Restaurant delivery services are a popular business that is often utilized by restaurant owners that are looking for alternatives to hiring their delivery drivers. Some of the reasons restaurant owners use a delivery company are:

- Low delivery volume

- No wireless debit machines available for delivery

- Exposure for a new restaurant to existing delivery clients

- A delivery company to coordinate the delivery times and hire drivers

- Elimination of delivery driver staffing problems

Benefits of Online Orders

1. Online orders are typically larger than orders that are phoned in. The customer has more time to browse over the menu items they would like to order, and they are prompted to add popular items along the way.

2. Language barriers between customers, the dispatcher, and the restaurant are highly reduced.

3. The restaurant's workflow is interrupted less often because they can review the order when it is more convenient. A customer standing at the cash register can take a higher priority than checking the email for a new online order.

Chapter 45– Start A Home Based Business By Providing Dog Walking Services

The services you can consider in offering to the people around your community is taking care of dogs or walking them.

When you take a look around your neighborhood, most likely, you will see a lot of households having their dogs, but the owners are too busy that some of them may not be able to take their dogs on their daily walks.

If you like dogs, then this would be a very profitable business you can get involved with. Keep in mind that household dogs do not get enough exercise, which is why they need to be walked. Therefore, begin offering your services, and their owners will surely be glad that you are willing to take care of their dog's daily walking activities.

With this kind of business, you need to know basic walking procedures, to ensure that the dog would be safe while he is with you. You do not want to compromise their safety, since their owners' love them, and you want to satisfy them with the kind of service you provide. Aside from that, they are your responsibility while they are with you.

To promote your dog walking home based business, you can always use flyers and even advertise on the web. Do not worry since dog lovers have friends who love dogs as well. Once you provide a high quality of service, they will be more than willing to spread the good word about you, and help you get more clients.

Chapter 46 – How to Make Extra Money Online With Getting Paid to Sites

Earning online can be difficult at first. There's so much information and it always seems as if you have actually to have your website to start. Many people don't have their websites and are earning hundreds of dollars every month with "get paid to" sites.

Some people choose not to take the money and decide that they would rather take the gift and give it to a family member or friend.

So how exactly do these sites work? People believe that money can never be completely free. And most of the time they're correct.

Get paid to sites don't give you free money. You're getting paid by the site to complete offers - the site gets paid when you complete offers - therefore the site can pay you from the money that they make.

It's simple. Some sites give you a choice whether you would sign up with them as a referral or points account. Referral accounts mean when you sign up you complete an offer and then refer friends to the site and have them complete an offer for you - therefore earning free money or gifts through your friends.

Chapter 47 – Get Paid to Be Online

Most internet users do the same things while they are online. They do stuff like read emails, chat with friends, visit websites, participate in forums, and play games. These are everyday things that a majority of internet users do without realizing they can make money doing those things. You can get paid to be online.

If you want to earn money for reading emails, you can easily do that. There are several websites out there where you can sign up to receive cash emails sent to your inbox.

All you have to do after that is open the emails to get credit for them. You will not get rich doing this, but it can be a good source of extra income.

Chapter 48 – Online Competitions - How to Make Money From It

More and more people are indulging themselves in making money online. Some are searching for ways on how to do this quickly by signing in to certain jobs and some would opt to do this the easier way, and that is through joining online competitions.

Many have chosen to get themselves involved with doing it the hard way.

However, some find it a bit more exciting to join certain competitions on the web and earn money from there. More often these kinds of deals are money that you can earn for quite a shorter period.

Many have been asking themselves how they would be able to earn money in an easier way without having to spend the much money for performing certain tasks online.

Some would opt to join competitions online because this is much easier compared to taking advantage of other online job opportunities that will also allow them to earn more money.

There are a lot of online competitions to join and more often these contests just a bit of understanding for more people to join in as well as easier mechanics to follow unlike when you are to take part in offline competitions.

One of the easiest competitions that you may come across will ask you to choose the right answer from a multiple choice question and then fill up some other required fields to make it possible for you to be a legitimate winner.

To make sure that you can surely take advantage of such competition offers online, you must be able to get yourself involved in as many competitions online as you can.

Chapter 49 – Become an Uber Partner Driver

You can start making money today as a Uber driver if you enjoy and know the best routes in town.

An Uber driver is a person who is self-motivated and can easily set his schedule since you are free when doing your work without a follow-up.

The payment offered is 20% to the Uber, and the remaining 80% goes to your pocket.

A person is required to own a four-door car, have no past criminal record, a driving license which is clean, driving experience of 3 years, and be 21 years of age.

Chapter 50 – Downloading Apps

There many companies that pay people to download an app and they are paid for every month that the keep the app in their phones. This is an appropriate way of making money online.

The company can easily understand the usage by the mobile and web better, e.g., the sites people enter, the popularity of the apps, the duration people use the app, and what is browsed by people on the web.

The following are the companies paying people to keep an app on their phones;

-Smart panel

-MobileExpressions for Android

-Shop tracker

Conclusion

There is nothing more tempting than the thought of making money online. Not every method will work for every one. Patience is the virtue you need to achieve success online.

Making money online is the life principle in its truest form. What worked yesterday may not work today, heck, it may not work fifteen minutes from now. If you are rigid, you will not maintain a successful online business.

If you are going to learn to make money online and be successful at it. You have to get a plan and stick with it for more than a few days. Making money online cannot be accomplished any other way. It will not be an overnight sensation, but with a bit of effort and a good business plan, you can say good-bye to that backbreaking job you now have.

The advertisers of all of those get rich quick schemes would have you believe it is as simple as "point and click" while that is certainly apart of it you have to do a bit more than that. The steps you take measure success.

The disclaimers tell the rest of the story. You begin to set hat you have to buy certain things and do certain actions for the programs to be of any use to you at all.

A lot of people will readily invest hundreds for the latest online money making scheme simply because it promises to make them success without them having to do more than make up a pass word. They sell you ebooks with steps to take but with little actual knowledge about how to implement those steps.

Research the program before you buy. If the person claims they have a million-dollar site, then visit it. See for yourself if this person is a fraud or not. There are those out there that are selling practical help to get you started in an online business these are the ones willing to lean over your shoulder and teach you step by step how to succeed.

Making money online seems like a way to get rich with no effort. This simply is not the way it works.

A lot of making money online advertisements would have you believe that you just pay a small fee and the money will start rolling in. Remember nothing in, nothing out is the rule. You have to play a part in your success.

The business model you choose will mean the difference in success and failure of your business. Making money online is not a hard task it just takes knowledge and persistence.

The steps you take measure success. Making money online often hinges on having a site that is both noticeable and easy to navigate. Research the program before you buy. If the person claims they have a million-dollar site, then visit it. If you are spending money for training having access to a live person makes all the difference.

Your business only grows if people are aware that it is there.

www.ingramcontent.com/pod-product-compliance
Lightning Source LLC
Chambersburg PA
CBHW070107210526
45170CB00013B/778